SEVEN
QUALITIES
WISE MEN
WANT

KINGSLEY OKONKWO

7 QUALITIES WISE MEN WANT

Printed in Nigeria by:
Living proof Press Ltd.
Tel: +234 802 389 1766
E-mail: livingproofpress@yahoo.com

To contact the author:
Tel:08077714411,08077714413

CONTENTS

Introduction

Have you ever seen a couple and wondered "What on earth brought these two people together?" Or you meet a beautiful woman and when she introduces her husband, you ask yourself, "What did she see in him? It is not what she saw in him, it is what she heard from him. Women are moved by words. Any man who can say the right things confidently to a woman stands a good chance of getting the most beautiful or sophisticated woman to marry him. It is however not so with men. Men are moved by what they see. For a man to pay attention long enough to be interested in all the virtuous qualities a woman has, he has to first like what he sees. This is why beautiful women have all kinds of men attracted to them. The men may eventually discover that these women don't have anything beyond their physical beauty to offer but they would have been distracted by her looks long before they get the chance to assess her content.

This is a book for men, but I know ladies are curious to know what men want so if you are a woman reading this, please don't focus on developing your inner qualities alone, invest also in your physical qualities. Like they say, "looking good is good business."

It's a common mistake for godly women to assume that loving the Lord, being intelligent and resourceful is all that is needed to get married to a good man so they pay little attention to how they look. The truth is, God made the woman beautiful both inside and outside. The

Bible has several references to the physical beauty of a woman. (See *Genesis 12:19, Genesis 29:17 and Genesis 26:7-9.*) Even businesses and companies are known to rely on good packaging to make their products and services attractive to their potential customers. If they don't do this, the average customer would walk past their products on the shelves and reach out for the more attractive but lower quality items. Personally, I will not look at a poorly packaged item twice. I believe that if the content is valuable, the manufacturers would have invested in wrapping it up nicely. It is important to look good.

However, as a man searching for a life partner, you must look beyond the physical beauty of a woman. The Bible clearly says, *"beauty is vain." (See Proverbs 31:30)* From a distance, a woman's beauty can be quite appealing and desirable but it doesn't count for much in marriage. There must also be inner beauty (character, virtues, and good qualities) at the core of the beautiful packaging you are admiring. For instance, a woman's physical beauty will not keep you faithful in the marriage. Many beautiful women, celebrities and models, have been cheated on, physically abused and divorced by their spouses. What a lasting marriage thrives on is real love; the kind of love that is beyond mere beauty or physical attraction.

I once counselled a man who shared some very bad things a lady did to him. From his story, it was obvious that the woman didn't care about him but he was too in love with her to notice. When I tried to get him to understand what the real issue was he quickly replied, "But Pastor I love her and I want to marry her." So, I asked him what he loved so much about her and he said, "Pastor, she is very beautiful." The young man was so stuck on the lady's beauty that he wasn't thinking straight anymore. As a man, you need to watch out for this. Samson was in love with Delilah. But, did Delilah love Samson? No. Was Delilah a good woman? No, she wasn't. Yet, the Bible recorded that Samson loved her and that led to his destruction. *(See Judges 16:4)*

In life, you will meet women you are drawn to either because of the way they talk or the way they look. There will also be times when you just like a woman for no specific reason but if you know the qualities to look out for, you will be able to know regardless of how you feel about her if she is right for you or not.

As a man, it is exciting when you find a woman you can have an intelligent conversation with. However, enjoying her company and finding it easy to talk with her does not mean both of you will make it in marriage. There is more to marriage than being able to hold an intelligent conversation. Marriage is about serving your purpose as a spouse in someone's life.

I once saw the advert for a very beautiful car, and I loved it. When I finally saw the car physically, I liked everything about it and wanted to buy it. But as I began to research on the features of the car, I discovered that I was not compatible with the car. It had some features that could not serve me in the ways I needed a car to serve me at the time. So, as you may have guessed, I didn't buy that car in spite of how I felt about it. I had to move from just my feelings to consider the functionality of the car. The same principle applies to marital relationships. It is one thing to like someone but an entirely different thing for you to be able to walk together as one in marriage.

In this book, I will be sharing those qualities you should look out for, and I pray that as you open your heart and mind to learn, there will be a renewal of your thought processes and an improvement in your value system so that you can walk into the glorious marital destiny with the right person God has prepared for you.

1

The Fear of the Lord

Favor is deceitful and beauty is vain but a woman that fears the Lord shall be praised.

PROVERBS 31:30 [KJV]

The first quality a wise man should look out for in a woman is the fear of the Lord. And this is by no means suggests being "crunchy". I have noticed over time that what people mean when they say a woman fears the Lord is that she goes to church regularly, carries the Bible everywhere she goes, attends every prayer

—

meeting, and participates in other religious activities.

But that is not what it means to have the fear of the Lord. A woman who fears the Lord, according to the Bible, is one who has a living and active relationship with God. This means that she loves God and is willing to obey His word above her personal opinion. I will tell you a simple but highly underestimated truth: your marriage will be sustained by your personal relationship with God and not by your relationship with your wife. This is not to say that you should not have a good relationship with your wife, you should, but your relationship with God must supersede that by a very wide margin.

Joseph had the chance to sleep with Potiphar's wife, but he said, "How can I do this great wickedness and sin against *God."(See Genesis 39:9)*. He wasn't worried about Potiphar finding out.

Potiphar would not have known that he was sleeping with his wife if Joseph had yielded to that temptation, but he did not give in because he had the fear of God. That singular choice, though it had some temporal unfavourable consequences for him, *(See Genesis 39:19-21)* preserved his life and destiny. You need to know that the only lasting motivation your wife will have to be faithful to you is her fear of God. It is a principal quality.

My wife does not submit to me because I say so or because I always do what she likes. She submits to me because the Bible instructs a woman to submit to her husband as the head of the home *(See Ephesians 5:22)* and that is exactly what my wife has been doing since we got married. Her submission to me is simply an expression of her obedience to the word of God. The woman is not meant to submit to her husband because she believes or agrees with everything he says. She is to submit to him as an obedience to God's instructions.

The Bible also instructs the man to love his wife. *(See Ephesians 5:25)* This means that you will put her needs first before yours. There will be times when you won't feel like doing certain things for her but because you fear God and you want to honour Him, you will do them regardless of how you feel. If the woman you want to marry is doing everything for you because she loves you, you must realize that a day will come when she will not be very pleased with you. And on such days, if there is no higher reason why she is with you apart from how she feels about you, you will not like how she will treat you.

It is always to your advantage when someone treats you right out of their fear of God than out of their love for you because that love may not always be there. Everyone needs someone they can trust to treat them right whether they feel like it or not. I heard of a case where a woman was giving birth to her child at the hospital while her younger sister was at home delivering another service to her husband. Clearly, the sister would pretend to be good when her elder sister is around but when she is gone, she will show her real character.

I live right because I want to honour God. There are a lot of things I could do that my wife may never get to know about, but God would know, and God is the one I am living for. I treat my wife with love and respect because God says I should. It never crosses my mind to treat her otherwise. This is not because of who she is or because I like her, even though she is an amazing person, my best friend and I'm absolutely in love with her. If your reason for not hurting your wife is that you like her, the day she offends you, you will beat her up because the human part of you would want to get back at her. But if you treat her with respect because you honour God, no matter what she does to you, you will want to stand in righteousness before God. That way, raising your hands against her will never be an option.

You need to know that my wife and I both had the fear of God before we met each other. Our relationship with God existed long before either of us came to know the other. So, before you ask that lady to marry you answer these questions,

"Does she love God?"

"Does she respect God?"

"Would she obey the word of God in spite of the situation she finds herself in or would she stubbornly stick to her own ways?"

Your partner cannot be going to church because of you. It is not sustainable. Look for a woman who is ruled by the Spirit of God and the Word of God because those are the things that will sustain your marriage. You need to come to terms with the fact that your spouse will not always please you. She will not always do what you like.

Many divorcees today were very happy on their wedding day, yet their marriages ended in a divorce. At some point in the marriage, the feelings they had for each other finished and they got tired of each other. But if pleasing God was their number one priority, they would have been willing to do the right thing for their marriage in obedience to God's word. So when you hear people who are supposed to be Christians say, "I am tired of my marriage. I want a divorce." You can tell that they don't quite honour God in their hearts.

A certain man was very upset with his wife. He told her he didn't love her anymore and wanted to end their marriage. The case got to their pastor, and he paid them a visit. After speaking with the couple, the pastor said to the man "Brother, you know the Bible says, "Husbands, love your wife." *(See Ephesians 5:25)* The man retorted, "She is not my wife anymore. She lives in the next room, so she is my neighbour." Then the Pastor replied, the Bible also says, "Love your neighbour as yourself." *(See Mark 12:31)* The man replied angrily, "She is not even my neighbour. We have not spoken to each other for the past three months. She is my enemy." The Pastor smiled and said, "Dear brother, the Bible also says, "Love your enemies and pray for them." *(See Mathew 5:44)*. After this the man kept quiet, he had nothing more to say. You see, there is no logical escape route in marriage when you do it God's way, which is why you must ensure that you choose the right person.

If you have been loving your enemies and your neighbours as God has commanded us to do, you will not find it difficult to love your wife, especially when she is not in her best behaviour. Living with your wife will not be hard if obeying the word of God has been your lifestyle. The Word of God remains the foundation for a successful relationship. Stay away from anyone who lacks the fear of God. If she does not see anything wrong with disobeying the word of God, she will not see anything wrong with disobeying you.

2

A Meek and Quiet Spirit

Whose adorning let it *not be that outward adorning of plaiting of hair and wearing of gold or of putting on of apparel but let* it *be the hidden man of the heart that which* is *not corruptible, even the ornament of a meek and quiet spirit which* is in *the sight of God of great price.*

- **1ST PETER3:3-4 [KJV].**

God places great value on a meek and quiet spirit and if God values a thing, it is wise for you to value it too. A meek and quiet spirit is essential. The New

International Version refers to it as the unfading beauty of a gentle and quiet spirit. This virtue never gets old or out of fashion. It is incorruptible and peaceful. Meekness literally means strength under control. It implies true humility. A meek woman would not oppose you or disrespect you even when she disagrees with or is yet to understand something you want her to do. She will submit to you and understand later. A woman who lacks this quality will be difficult to teach and therefore impossible to lead. She would rather hold on to her own ideas and opinions. You can't lead a woman who will not listen to you or learn from you. Communication is key in marriage. A follower must be open to receive instructions and willing to obey them. So, find out if the woman you are about to marry is willing to follow your lead.

Lot's wife is a good example. She became a pillar of salt because she refused to listen to simple instructions from the angel of God *(See Genesis 19:26)*. She knew that her husband was leaving Sodom and Gomorrah in obedience to the instructions given to them by the angels, yet she disobeyed and reaped the negative consequences of disobedience.

The man is the head of his home and the leader of his household. *(See 1st Corinthians 11:3)*. The right woman for you must be willing to submit to your leadership. A rebellious woman will nag and refuse to take correction but a woman who is willing to learn can develop to any level she wants in life. Stay away from a rebellious woman because she will not be a blessing to you.

On several occasions, a young man would walk up to me and say, "Pastor, there is a lady I want to marry. I have asked for her hand in marriage, but she doesn't want to accept my proposal. What do I do?" My response to that is always "If you cannot convince her to marry you, you won't be able to convince her to do any other thing or lead her in any other way."

One of the qualities I love the most in my wife is that she is very understanding. I could tell her something we are going to do at the spur of the moment, and she will listen and follow-through, even though it might not be convenient for her. It's easy for me to convince her to do something because she believes in me and understands our vision. I believe that when you marry the kind of wife you are supposed to marry, you will be able to explain anything to her.

Something happened when I was about to get married. My wife likes jewellery, especially rings. But when we got married, I couldn't afford to get her an engagement ring. I told her that the plan was not to get engaged to her but to marry her so what she needed from me was the wedding ring, not an engagement ring. As our wedding day drew near, my mother-in-law asked us if we were not going to print a wedding program. It was obvious that she had been expecting to see one for a while and since none had been sent to her, she had to ask us about it. I told her not to worry about it that everything would be fine on that day. But in my mind, I had reasoned that people don't keep wedding programs. Most times, after the wedding ceremony is over, the guests would simply drop it on the table or the floor and go their way. Also, the master of ceremony would always tell everyone what is coming up next so there was no need to print any program after all. I was not going to waste money we didn't have on something we didn't need. I explained this to my wife and told her that the only person who needed a wedding program was the Master of Ceremony, she thought that was a good idea and agreed to it.

So, marry someone you can communicate with easily. In life, there will always be seasons when you will need to make certain adjustments to accommodate the demands of a season till it's over. At such times, you don't need someone that will oppose you. You will want someone who will listen to you and work together with you to achieve your desired goals for your family. If you want to know the kind of person a woman is, you may ask her questions like, "Should we rent a house or buy a land and build? Should we live in a small place now while we save and work on building our own house tomorrow?"

Her answers will reveal her thought patterns and values.

Talking to your wife is your principal assignment as a man. You must have the ability to share your vision with her. You must be able to sell your ideas to her and she must be willing to buy into it wholeheartedly. God has made you the leader of your home, so lead.

3

Virtue

Who can find a virtuous woman?
Her price is far above rubies
PROVERBS 31:1 [KJV]

A virtuous woman is hard to find. She is of rare quality and inestimable value, she is priceless. The whole chapter of Proverbs 31 gives us a clear picture of the kind of person a virtuous woman is. She did not depend on a man to meet her needs or pay her bills. She was very hardworking and involved in a lot of businesses. She was into real estate; she considered a piece of property and bought it. She was a philanthropist; she was renowned for her generosity to the poor. She was a skilled homemaker; her children and husband were well cared for. She was a human resource person and administrator; her staff had their tasks spelt out daily. She was an amazing chef; she sourced her spices from afar. She was a fashion designer; she made beautiful gowns and sold them. All the clothing of her family was handcrafted by her. If that woman was to live in our time, she would have several business cards with her name as the Managing Director or Chief Executive Officer of each of her companies.

With all her wonderful capabilities, only one thing was mentioned about her husband. He was at the gate of the city doing only one thing: deliberating on matters of state. I believe he was a politician, perhaps a local government chairman. But the virtuous woman could multitask. She juggled a lot of responsibilities and did them well.

In contrast, the average woman is out there looking for men to foot her bills. You don't need to search to find her. Just be willing to give her some money or take her out, and she will find you herself and give you her full attention. If only she knew who she was and her capacity to do great things, she will not be out on the streets selling herself short. It's a sad reality that many women don't know their worth and how powerful they are. They don't know how gifted they are.

As a young boy, my mother would wake me and my brothers up early in the morning (we are five boys in all). She would cook breakfast for all of us, dress us up for the day and do many other things she had to do before her day starts. Yet, she managed to still be on time to join my father as they leave for work. All I could remember my father do was wake up, had his bath, eat and meet her at the car. My father did not bother himself with household chores. He knew that my mother had that under control. She was great at multitasking. A woman can be talking on the phone, watching a soap opera, breasting-feeding, and cooking all at the same time. Most men will not try that, they can only do one thing at a time. Talking to a man when he is watching a football match, for instance, is a waste of time. He will not hear a word of what you are saying. The virtuous woman lived her life productively on her own. She was so blessed that she supported her husband with ease, contributing substantially to the welfare of her family. Her sense of purpose made her attractive. She was careful to marry a man whose vision could accommodate hers. She depended on God alone and lived an extraordinary life. Marriage only enhanced her capacity to achieve her goals and dreams.

These days, it is difficult to find a woman with dreams. Quite a number of women in this part of the world have only one desire in life and that is to get married. I always advise young women to do something with their lives and have big dreams. God has put incredible potentials in men and women, it is up to us to release them.

God never asks us to do what He knows we cannot do. He gifted everyone with the capacity for what they should be doing. It is true that a man can make a woman's life better, but it is important to realize that within her is a God-given ability to be great on her own. If only women worldwide will place as much value on their personal development as they do on the latest fashion trends like clothes, bags, shoes and hair, they will not struggle so much with low self-esteem. The reason many women would invest so much on themselves (what they wear and how they look) than in themselves (being a better person) is because they try to get their sense of worth from material things. This is why some of them would dance suggestive dances in musical videos for a small amount of money. My heart breaks whenever I see such things. I wish I could tell those women that they are made for much more than embarrassing themselves to earn a living. Think about it, how much could a *"Sugar Daddy"*, or what we refer to as *'Aristo'* in this part of the world, possibly give to a woman that is worth her virtue? I'm yet to hear of any woman who received an award for having the most benevolent sugar daddy as a sponsor. No, you won't hear of any such thing because there is no future in that lifestyle. The only thing you will find at the end of it is destruction and death.

> *There* is *a way that seems right to a person, but eventually* it *ends in death.* -PROVERBS 14:12 [GWT]

There are women you can't even imagine to ask to do such belittling things because you know that with the kind of job they have or the kind of businesses they run, they can hire you if they want to. Thank God for women like Tara Fela-Durotoye who own their own businesses.

Don't marry a liability. A greedy and lazy beautiful woman will leave you for someone else who can cater to her expensive tastes better than you can. I must mention that there are a few odd men who prefer to marry a liability because it makes them feel powerful that a woman is totally dependent on them. But I believe you are not that kind of man so look out for a virtuous woman. You will know her by her values; what she says and what she is excited about.

Wisdom

Every wise *woman builds her house, but the foolish plucketh* it *down with her own hands.*

PROVERBS 14:1 [KJV]

Wisdom is the ability to know the truth and live by it. Matthew 7:24(NIV) says,

"Therefore, everyone who hears these words of mine *and puts them* into *practice* is *like a* wise *man who built his house on the rock.*

A wise woman is a woman who practices the truth she knows; she builds her home on spiritual principles.

A foolish woman destroys her own home with her own hands, and I have seen many women do this. Sometime ago a couple of angry women came together and formed a group against men. They felt that submitting to their husbands was wrong and men had no right to demand respect from them. However, what they failed to realize was that God made men that way intentionally and it's not a woman's responsibility to try to change a man. It wasn't a man's idea that his wife should respect and submit to him, God commanded it to be so. *{See Ephesians 5:33)* And a wise woman will obey that instruction because it is for her own good.

It is important to note here that a woman

plays a very unique role in the life of her husband and God equipped her specially for that work. He gave her the ability to influence her husband. This makes her very powerful. A wise woman can respect her husband into doing what she wants him to do without having to fight with him over it. She knows the value of simple things that can keep her marriage. For instance, she knows that men are moved by what they see so she takes care of herself and looks good for her husband like the virtuous woman did. *(See Proverbs 31:22)* She knows that responding gently soothes angry feelings *(See Proverbs 15:1)* so she speaks in a manner that will not stir up strife or quarrel in her home. Unfortunately, many women think they should always talk back when a man talks to them. But that's not wise at all. So, look out for how she talks to you.

Abigail was a wise woman. *(1st Samuel 25)*. She was married to a man named Nabal which meant *fool*. In the story, David was on his way to kill Nabal and his household for something foolish he did in a drunken state and her servants told her about it. Knowing the kind of man she was married to and the risk involved in waiting for David to get to her household in anger, she came up with a strategy to stop David from carrying out his threats on her family. David had asked Nabal for some food for himself and his men, but Nabal turned him down and insulted him, so she quickly prepared a generous amount of food and went to meet David. When she met him, she humbled herself and spoke to him with deep respect. She referred to David as Lord fourteen times while addressing him. This was the same David that her husband had referred to as a runaway slave. Somehow, she had information concerning David's calling and future and was quick to respectfully remind him that a man of his calibre and anointing must not soil his hands with the blood of a foolish man like her husband. With that singular act, she saved her family and left a lasting impression in the heart of David such that after Nabal died, David did not waste time to get married to her.

A wise woman would seek to know what her husband or fiancé's vision is. Some women do not know what their husbands' goals and dreams are. A woman cannot pray for her husband effectively without that information.

Look for a woman who has developed her intellectual capacity. If you are a banker, for instance, you would like a woman who knows something about banking. You will want to take her along to hang out with your friends because you are proud of her, and you know she can hold intelligent conversations with them. I am always relaxed when my wife needs to represent me somewhere because there is practically no subject you want to discuss that she won't be able to contribute constructively to. In fact, sometimes I even take her along to places to protect myself because I might not know some of the things that will be discussed. But I know some men who find it difficult to take their wives to any intellectual gathering because when she talks, she will expose her ignorance. This is why some men would hide their wives because they don't want to be embarrassed. So, look out for a woman who has developed her intellectual capacity- a wise woman!

5

Hospitality

And having a reputation for good works: if she has brought up children, has shown hospitality, has washed the feet of the saints, has cared for the afflicted and has devoted herself to every good work.
1ST TIMOTHY 5:10 [KJV]

A man is happy when his friends visit and his wife can host them cheerfully. Women have the natural ability for hospitality. The only limitation is that some women have not taken the time to develop it. You need a hospitable woman as a wife because a need will always arise for your wife to entertain guests on short notice. A hospitable woman will raise your children, run the home, and supervise your house-helps. You do not want a home where the help is a threat to your children because your wife does not treat her well.

The Bible says that while entertaining strangers, one day we might entertain angels *(See Hebrews 13:2)*. Hospitality was how Rebecca got to marry Isaac. She saw an elderly man and treated him with kindness. She did not only give him a drink, she also gave his camels water as well *(See Genesis 24:18-19)*. It is said that a thirsty camel can drink more than thirty gallons of water in less than fifteen minutes. Some single women are only nice to men they see as eligible bachelors and they treat every other person poorly.

So, find out if she is friendly and nice to other people.

Marry a woman that has basic home skills like cooking because the average man is moved by what he eats. If she can't cook, she should learn how to. Not knowing how to cook is only a problem when you are not willing to learn. Today, a good cook is not just someone who knows her way around the kitchen or someone who can recreate her mother or grandmother's favourite recipe. A good cook is one who is creative in the kitchen and is willing to try out new recipes. This is a very important skill in these days of interracial and intertribal marriages.

Men like good food. A woman called me many years ago to report that her husband beat her up. I asked her what the problem was and she said she served his food late so he got upset and beat her up. If you know that food is very important to you, please do not marry a woman who cannot cook. However, there are men who don't like food. They only eat because they have to or because they are forced to. For a man in this category, bread is food. But for some of us, bread, cereals, noodles and sandwich are not classified as food. It is just snacks or appetizers. We expect that real food is coming after it.

If a man pays his friend a visit and observes the exceptional way his friend's wife keeps the home and runs her household, he will take note of it. If the friend's wife is also a good cook and very hospitable, he will be impressed by it. When he gets home to his wife and the dinner served is not so good, he will begin to compare it with what he had for lunch at his friend's house. This by the way is a breeding ground for conflict.

Know your relationship with food and marry accordingly.

6

Wholesome

*Dear friend, I hope all **is** well with you and that you are as healthy **in** body as you are strong **in** spirit.*
3RD JOHN 1:2 [NLT]

In our world today, women suffer a lot in the hands of untrained men. There are many broken and hurting women everywhere and some struggle with low self-esteem as a result of what they have been through. If the woman you are about to marry had a painful past and is yet to recover from it, that's an emotional baggage and it will put a lot of strain on your marriage. *As* they say, *"A hurting person will hurt other people." A* woman with an unresolved past needs the help of the Holy Spirit to heal both emotionally and physically. And then, she needs to engage the service of a professional counsellor who would walk her through the process of healing.

The responsibilities of marriage can only be carried by individuals who are whole and sound. A woman with an emotional baggage cannot meet the demands of marriage. For instance, if she has been fighting all her life, she will see everything you do as confrontation and will always be battle ready for you. If she had an ex that cheated on her, she will be suspicious of you. If she hates herself because of what happened to her, she won't be able to love you wholeheartedly. That's just how it works.

Marry a woman who has gotten over her past experiences, has good self-esteem and loves herself. The scriptures say love your neighbour as yourself *(Mark 12:31)*. Don't be deceived, a woman needs to first love herself before she can love you. You can help her go through the healing process but don't marry her while she is still in the process. Let her heal.

There are ladies who are prone to fighting because they had a bad relationship with the authority figures in their lives. It could be an absentee father, an uncle or an older brother they despise for one reason or the other. So, they express their pain or hurt in the form of rebellion against any male figure they meet whether it is their boss, their pastor, their lecturer, etc. A woman like this will hate any form of authority over her and as her husband you are not exempted. She will resist your leadership because she has been conditioned to do so. In order words, until a woman deals with her past and let go of all her baggage, please don't take the friendship to the next level. If you love her, support her as she gets the help she needs.

Interestingly, some men are attracted to abused women. They believe that getting married to these women is a way of rescuing them from their troubles. I remember a particular young man who felt this way about a woman. He assumed that no man would want to marry her because of her terrible past and as such he decided to marry her. He did not realize that you don't have to marry everyone that enters your life. Some of the people in your life are there for you to help. It is wrong to marry anyone out of pity. Pity cannot sustain a marriage.

Be careful of rebound relationships. Some people are quick to jump into a new relationship as a means of getting over a heartbreak. That is one of the wrong reasons to enter a relationship. If you had a bad experience, you need to get over it, let go of unforgiveness and trust God to connect you with the right person at the right time.

7

Trustworthy

> *The heart of her husband doth safely trust* **in** *her so that he shall have* **no** **need** *of spoil.*
>
> **PROVERBS 31:11[KJV]**

Trust is the foundation of any lasting marriage. If you cannot trust a woman and she doesn't trust you, you have nothing in common. There's a general notion that men are prone to cheating in relationships more than women, but you will be amazed at the number of women who are cheating on their husbands or fiancés these days.

Statistics show that in about sixty percent (60%) of the families who took part in the Immigration DNA Test at the embassy, at least one child belonged to the mother but had no paternal link to the father. This is why you have to marry someone you can trust. The Bible says, *a gracious woman will retain her honour (See Proverbs 11:16).* A woman who cheats on her husband will also lie to him to cover her tracks.

A long time ago, I was standing outside a bank in Festac, Lagos when I noticed a beautiful woman dressed in a corporate attire. She was on the phone with someone who I believe wanted to know where she was and she said she was somewhere in Oshodi, an entirely different location from where we were. I was shocked. We were in Festac, yet she said she was in Oshodi. Where was her integrity? Yet someone will marry her with that character flaw unchecked. There is no such thing as a "white lie". Watch out for the woman who is quick to lie to cover up for you. You may think she is such a good person who cares about you, but the reality is you are training her to lie to you when the need arises. Anyone who lies for you will someday lie to you or lie against you.

I once heard of a man who asked his friends in the telecommunications industry to download all the numbers his wife called within a certain period. He wanted to know all the places she had been to and even called those places to confirm. There was also the case of a man who would call his wife and after speaking with her would insist on speaking with the friend she went to visit to confirm her current location. What a pity. You may be amused by this example but without trust in your relationship, you will not be able to sleep at night and you will not have peace of mind.

Being a person of integrity is important before and after marriage. There are families where the husband and wife don't know each other's assets. They hide their money and their salaries from each other. The man has a house, and the woman is building her own but neither of them is aware of what the other is doing.

Trust is a vital part of any relationship, not just only in marriage. You need trust in your dealings with other people as well. When you say that something is a certain way, your wife or fiancée should be able to take your word to the bank. And if you do not have that kind of confidence in the woman you are about to marry then you need to work on building your level of trust. This is vital to the success of any marital relationship.

It wasn't a coincidence that Mary the mother of Jesus Christ was a virgin. Imagine if she was not a virgin before she became pregnant by the Holy Spirit. Do you know the kind of controversy that would have been generated? Some men would be glad she didn't mention their names but there will always be some who would come out boldly just to refute her claims even if they were true. That's why God chose a virgin. It pays to live a holy life. Marriage does not stop sexual pressures or temptations if anything, it amplifies it. Self-control is important. The same line you cross to commit fornication is the same line you will cross to commit adultery. In Galatians 5:19-21, the first two works of the flesh to be listed were adultery and fornication. If you cannot control yourself from doing the wrong things now, why do you think you will be able to control yourself in marriage?

So, having discussed the seven qualities to look out for in a lady you intend to marry, it will also be to you benefit to understand how women are wired. Here, we will be highlighting some major differences between men and women.

SOME DIFFERENCES BETWEEN MEN AND WOMEN

Women are emotional beings. If a woman is talking to someone she likes, even when they are discussing trivial things like a tie, sunglasses, or shoes, she won't mind as long as they are talking. She will enjoy herself. Men, on the other hand are logical beings. A man wants to have a rational and meaningful conversation and he likes a woman that can stimulate him mentally. Talking is not as easy for men as it is for women. They would rather spend more time thinking than they do talking. A man can sit quietly and think for hours and be fulfilled but a woman might not be able to do that.

Women think out loud, but men think within. Women are natural talkers while men are natural thinkers. A woman might be processing what she is saying while she is talking but a man would rather finish thinking on it before he talks about it. Men don't talk for fun like a woman would. From childhood, you will notice that female children start talking earlier than peace of mind as a man that you marry a woman who is wise and understands these things.

Conclusion

In choosing the right partner, you need the right values and expectations. Be conscious of the qualities we discussed in this book as it will help you choose the right woman for you. It will also be an added benefit if you read the sequel to this book – *7 Questions Wise Women Ask.* It will help you know if you are the right person for her. Having this knowledge base will position you and your spouse for a blissful marriage.

I pray for you that as you apply the wisdom in this book, you will have the marriage of your dreams. You will not struggle in your marriage in Jesus' name. Amen.

Surrender To Christ

If you read through this book, then you know that a great marriage is a privilege of God's children. The only way to become a child of God is by giving your life to Christ. And if you haven't done that already, the best time to do so is now. You can say this prayer after me:

Lord Jesus, come into my heart. Forgive me my sin. Wash me with you blood. I receive the grace to serve you all the days of my life. Thank you, Father, for I am born again in Jesus mighty name, Amen.

Congratulations! Welcome to the family of God.

About The Author

Kingsley Okonkwo is a Specialist when it comes to Relationships and Marriages. With over two decades hands-on experience as a pastor, relationship coach, counsellor and best-selling author, PK, as he is fondly called is a presidential member of the American Association of Christian Counsellors, a board-certified Master Christian Life Coach, and a certified relationship counsellor. He is renowned for Love and Relationships, Marriage and Family Life, Domestic Violence, Divorce, and Infidelity Recovery.

He is the visionary behind the phenomenal *Love, Dating and Marriage Ministry,* widely known as ***LdmwithPK,*** a highly impactful relationship ministry with a reach of hundreds of thousands of people across the globe. Kingsley Okonkwo is committed to equip ping couples around the world with godly principles for building strong relationships and marriages having lived on the same principles himself for close to two decades. He is convinced that godliness is the foundation for quarrel-free marriages and as such hosts the *Together Forever* conference an annual Interdenominational event for married couples aimed at rekindling the passion and love in marriages.

Notably, his ministry records mind blowing testimonies of blissful relationships and marriages to the glory of God as more single people find the right partners, troubled marriages experience total restoration, individuals are delivered from sexual addictions and wrong mindsets redirected. His unique say-it-as-it-is, fun-filled style of teaching

God's principles for dating, courtship and marriage endears him to both the young and old as they are greatly impacted by his *relationship masterclasses, one-on-one coaching classes, live broadcasts* on social media and numerous *ministry resources.*

Pastor Kingsley continues to be a blessing across continents through itinerant relation- ship seminars, conferences and counsel- ling sessions across Canada, United States of America, United Kingdom, the Middle East, and numerous African countries. His messages and ministry materials are highly sought-after around the globe. He has authored numerous books on relationships, a few of which he co-authored with his lovely wife and partner in ministry, Pastor Mildred and they are blessed with three adorable children.

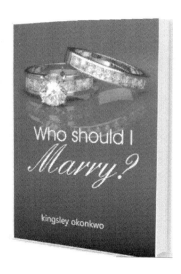

WHO SHOULD I MARRY?

Do you feel like you are literally faced with the option of choosing between the icing and the cake? If you are, then this book is for you. In it, you will discover the Ten Undeniable Qualities that will serve as a guide and "must- have" for your Mr. or Miss Right.

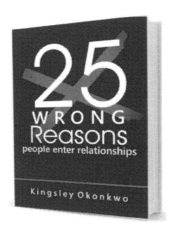

25 WRONG REASONS PEOPLE ENTER RELATIONSHIPS

If you marry for the wrong reasons, you will most likely marry the wrong person.

This insightful book will serve as a personal checklist for your motives as it highlights 25 reasons you shouldn't enter a relationship.

WHEN AM I READY?

- What must I attain, achieve and acquire to be considered ready?
- What are the basic things to look out for in a spouse?

These and more are clearly answered in the book, When Am I Ready? The striking truths in this book will not only make you know if you are ready for marriage but will also adequately prepare you for it.

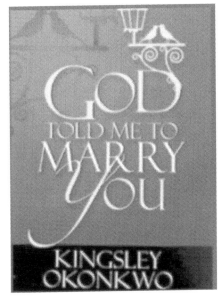

GOD TOLD ME TO MARRYYOU

In Christian circles today, this issue of "GOD SAID" or "GOD TOLD ME", has brought a lot of confusion and caused a lot of problems. The chapters in this book will clear out any doubt from your heart about "GOD SAID" or "GOD TOLD ME".

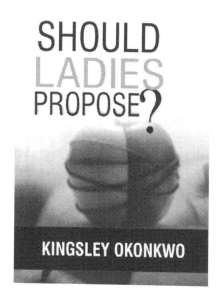

SHOULD LADIES PROPOSE?

This is one of the many controversial issues when it comes to relationships and in over a decade of speaking to youths and singles. It has turned out to be a constant question... do you need answers? Then this book is for you.

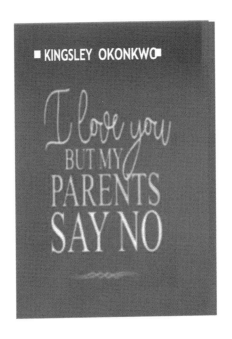

I LOVE YOU BUT MY PARENTS SAY NO

This mini-book helps to answer the pressing question of "How involved should your parents be in the selection of whom you marry?" and practical steps you can take when they object your choice.

WAITING FOR ISAAC

Contrary to what many say, God does not save the best for last; He always saves the best for the best times. He may not come when you want Him, but He is never late. This book is for every one that has ever asked "What do I do while I wait?"

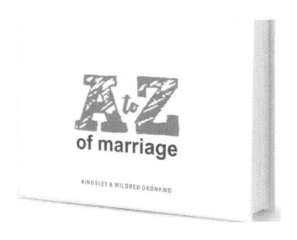

A TO Z OF MARRIAGE

A-Z of marriage is a matter of fact and very precise manual, alphabetically arranged for convenience, to help men and women better understand their needs for a better marriage.

HELP! MY HUSBAND IS ACTING FUNNY

Help! My husband is acting funny is a product of many years of counselling women going through tough times in their marriages. It provides clear, practical, and time-tested counsel that has changed the situation of numerous women.

ALL YEAR ROUND FOR MEN

ALL YEAR ROUND FOR MEN is a 52-WEEK GUIDE ON HOW TO LOVE YOUR WIFE. It is a practical, and easy-to-follow companion for the husband who wants to do right by his wife, making her feel special, loved and protected. It contains 52 tested and trusted tips to help you love your wife all year round.

MANUAL – THE WAY MEN THINK

A lot of women are stressed in relationships and marriages because they don't understand the way men think. This book addresses the psychology of men and also gives you practical tips you can leverage on.

HOW TO KNOW IF HE/SHE REALLY LOVES YOU

The author's passion in this book is to help you clarify if what you are feeling is love and also help you discover if what the person you love has for you is also love. So, if you are ready, let's discover, *"...if he or she truly loves you"*

OTHER BOOKS BY KINGSLEY & MILDRED OKONKWO

- When Am I Ready? Who Should I Marry?
- 25 Wrong Reasons People Enter Relationships.
- Just Us Girls
- I Love You but My Parents Say No
- Should Ladies Propose?
- God Told Me to Marry You
- Waiting For Isaac
- 7 Questions Wise Women Ask
- Chayil- The Virtuous Woman
- A-Z Of Marriage
- Help! My Husband Is Acting Funny
- All Year Round- For Men
- All Year Round- For Women
- Hannah's Heart Devotional
- Manual - The Way Men think.
- 21 Days Prayers and Fasting for Expectant Mothers. (e-book)
- One Thing
- God Can Be Trusted - Volume 1 & 2
- How to Know If He or She Really Loves You
- Praying for Your Husband
- Praying for Your Wife
- Common Love Lies that can stop you from finding true love.
- How to Make Love to a Woman without Touching Her
- No Dry Season - *A Devotional* on *Financial Prosperity* for *Couples.*
- 7 Things I Badly Want to Tell Women